50 GEM

Northumberland

STEVE ELLWOOD

AMBERLEY

First published 2018

Amberley Publishing
The Hill, Stroud
Gloucestershire, GL5 4EP

www.amberley-books.com

Copyright © Steve Ellwood, 2018

Map contains Ordnance Survey data © Crown copyright and database right [2018]

The right of Steve Ellwood to be identified as the Author
of this work has been asserted in accordance with the
Copyrights, Designs and Patents Act 1988.

British Library Cataloguing in Publication Data.
A catalogue record for this book is available from the British Library.

ISBN 978 1 4456 7907 5 (paperback)
ISBN 978 1 4456 7908 2 (ebook)

Origination by Amberley Publishing.

Printed in Great Britain.

Contents

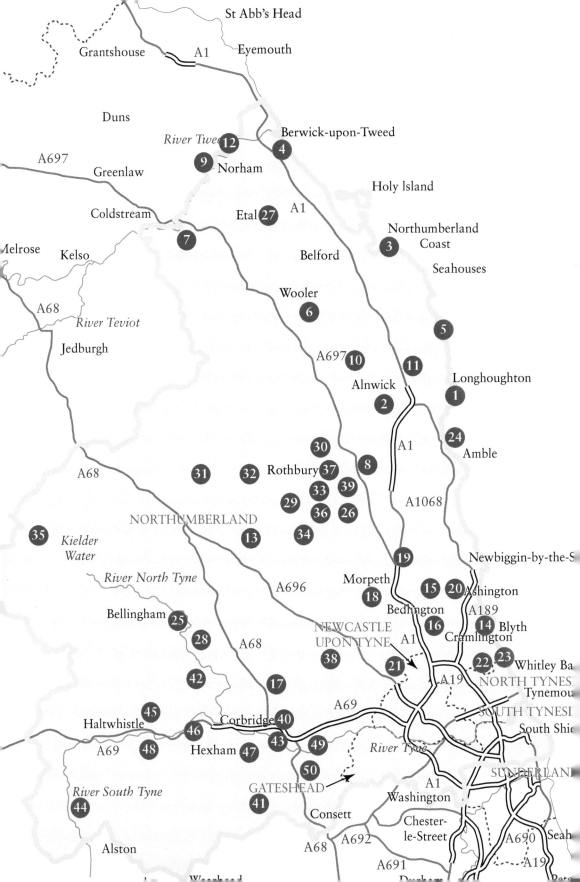

Introduction

This book is intended to highlight fifty gems of Northumberland, and so it is worth considering what a 'gem' is. The dictionary defines a gem as being 'a person or thing regarded as precious or special'. Hopefully I have selected fifty examples from Northumberland that illustrate the word 'gem' well, but it has to be said that there are many more within the county and I would urge the reader to seek them out.

The name of Northumberland (Northumbria) is derived from the Old English 'Norþan hymbra', translated as 'people or province north of the Humber'. In medieval times the kingdom of Bernicia under King Æthelfrith covered the area from north of the River Humber to the Firth of Forth. Nowadays the northernmost county in England, it borders Scotland to the north, Cumbria to the west and both Tyne and Wear and Durham to the south.

Militarily Northumberland has been much fought over, as it borders Scotland. The Roman General Hadrian in AD 122 decided to build his defensive border wall across the county running from Wallsend to the Solway Firth. Over the centuries numerous battles were fought not only between English and Scottish armies but also between the various Northumbrian lords and earls. This is one of the reasons why Northumberland was the site of many castles and fortifications, some of which still survive today, although mostly as ruins.

Geographically Northumberland is dominated by the Cheviot and Simonside Hills, which are located in the central part of the county. A flat coastal plain adjacent to the North Sea runs to the east of the county with some idyllic sandy beaches, rocky outcrops and cliffs. To the south-west lie the river valleys of the Tyne and the expansive man-made forests and reservoir at Kielder.

Covering an area of 5,013 square kilometres (1,936 square miles), Northumberland is the least densely populated county in England with a current estimation of 319,000 residents, half of whom live in the south-east of the county.

A popular visitor destination, tourism represents 11.8 per cent of Northumberland's economy, contributing £665 million. Transport links include the East Coast main rail line, the A1 north/south road, Newcastle Airport and the Port of Tyne, which has both a daily link with Amsterdam and a cruise ship terminal.

Whether your interest is in history, walking, bird and wildlife watching, outdoor sports, beach life or simply enjoying wide-open spaces, Northumberland is the place for you. By the way, Northumbrians are friendly people.

North

1. Alnmouth

The small picturesque village of Alnmouth lies at the mouth of the River Aln, and thus derived its name. The Aln rises in the Northumberland Cheviot Hills and runs eastwards into the North Sea.

To the east of the A1068 road the village gives the impression of being an island, access being over a bridge crossing the Aln. It is however built on a spit of land surrounded on three sides by water. A fine view of the village can be seen if travelling on the main East Coast Railway line between Newcastle upon Tyne and Edinburgh. Alnmouth railway station is a short distance from the village.

Parking is available in the well-signposted car park located beside the sea on the eastern side of the village. I found the best route to explore the village was to start at the southern end of Northumberland Street, this being the main street containing many interesting buildings.

Historically the village has existed since at least 1150 when the land was granted to the Sheriff of Northumberland, William de Vesci. His son, Eustace, was further granted a royal charter in 1207 to establish a port and market in the village. For many centuries the port enabled the export of grain and the import of timber.

The geographical position of Alnmouth on the course of the River Aln was to lead to the downfall of its port trade in the nineteenth century. During a storm on Christmas Eve 1806, the course of the river changed direction and gradually over the years shifting sands and accumulations of silt rendered the port too shallow for ships to ply their trade. The last recorded vessel to sail from the port was the brigantine *Joanna*, which departed in 1896 having delivered a cargo of timber from Scandinavia.

Evidence of the trade in grain can still be seen in the village – at one time there were up to sixteen granaries. One example is the Grade I-listed Hindmarsh Hall situated on Northumberland Street. Built as a granary in the early eighteenth century, it went on to be used as a corn exchange, a chapel and is now the village hall.

The harbour located on Riverside Road is now home to pleasure craft and a building of note is the former Ferryman's Hut. The hut is over a century old and was used by the ferryman, who would row travellers from one side of the Aln to the other. John Brown, the last ferryman, retired in the 1960s and the hut is now a free-to-enter museum exhibiting items of local historical interest.

Above: Hindmarsh Hall, a former granary.

Left: Former Ferryman's Hut.

2. Alnwick

Located just off the A1 road, 55 kilometres (34 Miles) north of Newcastle upon Tyne, is the medieval market town of Alnwick. There are a number of car parks within the town, all free but some requiring a parking disc that can be purchased from local shops or the Tourist Information Centre.

The name Alnwick is derived from Old English: Aln from the river on which it stands and Wic meaning 'dairy or farm'.

Home to the Earls of Northumberland, it is considered to be the traditional county capital town, although for administration purposes Morpeth is the headquarters of the county council.

The town is dominated by the Grade I-listed Alnwick Castle, which is adjacent to the River Aln. Home to the present (12th) Duke of Northumberland, Ralph Percy, it is also open to the public between April and September. Famous for its modern-day use by film makers, it has featured in *Blackadder*, *Robin Hood Prince of Thieves* and the *Harry Potter* series of films. The first known castle was built as a motte-and-bailey in the twelfth century by Gilbert Tyson, who acted as Standard Bearer to William the Conqueror at the Battle of Hastings in 1066. Built to defend the border between England and Scotland, it became stone built in 1138 when Eustace fitz John erected a more fortified building to defend against attacks from north of the border. It first came into ownership of the Percy family in 1309 when purchased by Sir Henry de Percy. A later Percy, Algernon,

Alnwick Castle from Lion Bridge.

Tenantry Column or Farmers Folly.

the 4th Duke, employed the architect Anthony Salvin to restore the castle back to its medieval state in 1852, and that is the building we see today.

Alnwick became a walled town in 1433 when a licence was obtained from Henry VI to enclose the town. The walls took some fifty years to complete, building costs being met by the local inhabitants and surprisingly with no contribution by the Earl of Northumberland. The Grade I-listed Bondgate Tower, also known as the Hotspur Tower, is evidence of the original town walls and stands on the main road into the town causing traffic to pass in single file. Another tower can be seen at Pottersgate, which was rebuilt in 1768 and is Grade II* listed.

The Grade I-listed Tenantry Column (also known as the Farmers Folly) stands at the west of the town and was built to honour Hugh, Duke of Northumberland. Designed by Newcastle architect David Stephenson, the Greek Doric column is 25 metres (85 feet) tall. The lions, notable for their straight horizontal tails, at the top and bottom of the column are part of the Percy family coat of arms. The building of the monument was funded by the tenants in gratitude to the 2nd Duke, who had lowered the rents of his tenanted agricultural workers in depressed times following the Napoleonic Wars. While it may be thought that the duke would feel honoured and thus amenable to his tenants, his reaction was to increase the rents, more than likely based on the fact that they obviously had money to spare, and consequently it became known locally as the Farmers Folly.

3. Bamburgh

Bamburgh can be accessed via the B1342 road, signposted from the A1 road, 85 kilometres (53 miles) north of Newcastle upon Tyne. There are a number of car parks provided in the village as well as considerate on-street parking. Bus services link Bamburgh from Berwick-upon-Tweed and Newcastle upon Tyne.

The name Bamburgh is thought to be derived from the Anglo-Saxon 'Bebba Burgh', Bebba being the wife of King Aethelfrith of Northumberland and 'burgh' being a fortified place.

The village is dominated by the Grade I-listed Bamburgh Castle which sits on top of a volcanic outcrop and has a number of other visitor attractions including the twelfth-century Church of St Aidan and the Grace Darling Museum. To suit the visitor there are a number of pubs, cafes, gift shops, galleries and holiday accommodation. The privately owned castle is open to the public between February and November, and an admission charge applies. Adjacent to the entrance is a car park for which a daily charge is made, but a free municipal car park can be found at the base of the castle at the side of the B1342 road.

Much of the castle's fabric dates from the twelfth century with extensive restoration having been carried out between 1894 and 1904 following its purchase by Lord William Armstrong, the Tyneside engineer and inventor. Employing the architect C. J. Ferguson, it was Armstrong's intention to

Bamburgh Front Street and Castle.

Grace Darling Memorial.

convert the castle into both a seaside family retreat and a convalescent home for retired gentlemen. Unfortunately Lord Armstrong died before the completion of the restoration and the castle remains in the ownership of the Armstrong family. The castle is open to the public and includes rooms such as the King's Hall, modified in Victorian times as a banqueting and ballroom with a false hammer ceiling made from Thailand teak. Also worthy of a visit is the Armstrong and Aviation Artefacts Museum, located within a building intended as a laundry for the convalescent home. It now houses exhibits detailing the Armstrong family achievements and also historical objects from the First and Second World Wars.

Grace Darling, the nineteenth-century heroine, was born in Bamburgh in 1815 and is recognised both by the Grace Darling Museum and also by a Grade II*-listed Gothic Revival-style monument in the churchyard of St Aidan's. Her father, William, was lighthouse keeper at the Longstone Light, which is situated on one of the Farne Islands. Grace and her nine siblings lived with their father and mother, Thomasin, on the island. On the evening of 7 September 1828 the paddle steamer *Forfarshire*, en route between Hull and Dundee, struck rocks on the Outer Farne. Despite heavy seas and darkness both Grace and her father rowed a Northumbrian coble boat in a valiant attempt to rescue the sixty-one passengers and crew. Their efforts led to the rescue of nine survivors, with nine others making their own way to the shore. Forty-three including the ship's captain, John Humble, and his wife, all perished.

4. Berwick

Lying at the northern tip of Northumberland is the English town of Berwick-upon-Tweed, reached via the A1 road or by train on the East Coast Line. The town is 4.8 kilometres (3 miles) from the Scottish border. For those travelling by road there are a number of free municipal car parks, although some do require parking discs.

The name Berwick is derived from the Old English 'Bere-wic', meaning 'Barley Farm'.

A fortified town with walls from two separate periods still on display, the medieval walls were commenced in the thirteenth century and the Elizabethan walls were built between 1558 and 1603. A section of the medieval walls can be seen close to the railway station and the Elizabethan defences encircle the town.

Sitting on the River Tweed and close to the North Sea, Berwick was an important town due to its strategic location and was much fought over in various Anglo-Scottish wars; indeed, the town changed hands on thirteen occasions, finally becoming English in 1482.

The town is compact and with a sturdy pair of shoes is easily examined on foot, but a word of advice would be to visit the Tourist Information Centre on Walkergate to obtain some guide booklets. Official walking tours can also be booked including an L. S. Lowry tour, which follows the locations used by the English artists in his numerous paintings and drawings of Berwick.

Marygate from Scots Gate.

Parade Square at Ravensdowne Barracks.

I would recommend the 3.2-kilometre (2-mile) walk around the Elizabethan walls, which gives a good view of the fortifications that protected the town. While access to the walls is free, I would suggest a visit to Ravensdowne Barracks, built in the early eighteenth century to garrison the many soldiers defending the town. Now under the guardianship of English Heritage, there is an entry charge to view the barracks and its three individual museums.

There is so much to see in Berwick and I would recommend a full day is allocated to take in its many historical features, which range from the military to fine architectural buildings. The town also has many independent shops, cafés and restaurants.

5. Dunstanburgh

Located on the Northumberland Coast overlooking the North Sea is the picturesque former fishing village of Craster. The village is accessible from Alnwick, 11 kilometres (7 Miles) by a bus service or by car via the B1340 road.

If travelling by vehicle there is a municipal car park on the road entering the village, signposted to the right-hand side and adjacent to the Tourist Information Centre. There is no public car parking in the village itself but it is only a short walk into Craster.

The meaning of Craster is derived from the Old English 'Crowchester', meaning 'Roman fort inhabited by crows' – evidence of Roman occupation was found at nearby Dunstanburgh Castle during works in the 1920s and 1930s.

Well known as the home of the Craster Kipper, the Robson family still smoke and cure herring in their smokehouse within the village. Kippers can be bought from the Robson's shop or enjoyed at the nearby restaurants.

The present harbour was built by the Craster family at the turn of the twentieth century to transport locally quarried stone (the car park mentioned above is in the former quarry), which was cut into kerbstones for use in London. The strange-looking tower at the end of the harbour was used to lift stones onto boats until the quarry closed in 1938.

Craster is also the starting point for a pleasant 2-kilometre (1.25-mile) walk over a sheep-grazing pasture to reach Dunstanburgh Castle. The pathway runs parallel to the rocky shoreline and is a fairly flat walk. While in a ruined state the castle on its elevated position makes an impressive sight as you walk from Craster.

The castle is Grade I listed, a Scheduled Ancient Monument and a Special Protection Area for the conservation of wild birds. Owned by the National Trust and managed by English Heritage, there is an entry charge. Built in 1313 by Thomas Earl of Lancaster, the castle was further fortified by John of Gaunt in 1380. The castle was abandoned as a garrisoned fortification in the fifteenth century and it went into steady decline, with stones being recycled in the construction of other Northumbrian castles and buildings. Entry to the site

Craster Harbour.

Approach to Dunstanburgh Castle from Craster.

is via the imposing Barbican Gatehouse, which can be entered and explored, a set of spiral stairs leading up to a viewing area giving marvellous views over the grounds and coastline. A walking route within the site takes the visitor around the castle walls and remaining towers as well as affording views of the many nesting seabirds at Gull Crags.

6. Edlingham

The small village of Edlingham lies to the immediate north of the Rothbury to Alnwick road (B6341). Car parking is available next to St John the Baptist Church, which is located on the right-hand side as you enter the village.

The name is derived from the Old English 'homestead of Eadwulf's people' and historical records show that a village has existed since at least 737. In that year the village was granted by King Coelwulf to Lindisfarne Monastery.

The Grade I-listed church dates mainly from the eleventh and twelfth centuries with additions and alterations from later periods. It was built on the site of an earlier Saxon wooden church. The present church is built from local grey sandstone, with a defensive tower and squat nave. It is thought that the three-stage tower was added in the thirteenth century in an attempt to offer protection to villagers from Scottish Raiders. It may also have been used to temporarily jail captured 'brigands'. The tower can only be accessed from the

Above: St John the Baptist Church.

Below: Remains of Edlingham Castle.

interior of the church, adding to its security. The church is open to the public and its interior is well worth viewing.

A short walk from the church stands the Grade I-listed Edlingham Castle, a fortified manor house, built between 1295 and 1300 for Sir William Felton, who was later to become Sheriff of Northumberland. In later periods defences such as a gatehouse and curtain walls were built to defend against raiders from the north. It ceased to be habitable in the seventeenth century when sacked by the Scots and much of its fabric was removed to erect local homes and farms. For centuries the castle lay abandoned, the majority of it covered in a grassy mound, only the tower visible to show it had existed. Following archaeological excavations during 1978 and 1982 the site was subsequently opened to the public with free entry and is under the guardianship of English Heritage. Many of the original buildings are now at foundation level, so a degree of imagination is required but noticeboards are present to help determine the various structures.

To the north-east of the castle lies the Grade II-listed Edlingham Railway viaduct, erected in 1885 to carry the North East Railway's Alnwick to Cornhill branch line across the Edlingham Burn. The line closed to passengers in 1930 and continued to be used by freight traffic up until its closure in 1953.

7. Flodden

The Battle of Flodden was fought between King James IV of Scotland and Thomas Howard, Earl of Surrey, on 9 September 1513 and is marked with a memorial cross to the west of the village of Branxton. The battlefield and the village are well signposted from the Morpeth to Coldstream A697 road.

A small car park is available at the foot of Branxton Hill, also known as Piper's Hill, and the monument is reached by a purpose-built pathway leading up a gentle slope. The walk to the monument gives views over the site on which the battle was fought as well as impressive views over the Northumbrian countryside and also into Scotland. The Grade-II polished-granite memorial cross was erected in 1910 by members of the Berwickshire Naturalists.

The cross commemorates those who perished in the battle: approximately 4,000 English and 10,000 Scots, including James IV. It is thought that the size of the two opposing sides was 30,000 Scottish soldiers and 26,000 English combatants, a conclusive and devastating result for both sides but more so for the Scots, who not only lost many troops but also their leader. It was a tremendous loss of life given that the battle lasted for only two hours.

Several information boards at the monument demonstrate the various aspects of how the battle was fought with maps, plans and explanations.

Above: Flodden Memorial Cross.

Below: Church of St Paul's, Branxton.

Close to Flodden Field and visible from Branxton Hill is the Grade II-listed Church of St Paul's, Branxton, dating from the twelfth century. After the Battle of Flodden the church was used as a temporary mortuary for King James IV and many of the other nobles who were slain. It is also thought that the churchyard contains many of the soldiers who lost their lives in the conflict. The church was largely rebuilt in 1849 to a Romanesque style but retains a twelfth-century chancel arch. Externally it is faced with volcanic dark brown rhyolite with sandstone dressing. During my visit the church was publicly open.

8. Ford

The small village of Ford lies on the B6353, which can be accessed from either the A1 or A697 roads. The place name is self-explanatory, as this was a fording place on the River Till, which is a tributary of the River Tweed.

The earliest recorded mention of Ford is in 1288 when Baron Muschamp granted land to Odinal de Ford to build a fortified house. In the same century the adjacent Church of St Michael and All Angels was built.

Much of the residential parts of the village were built as a 'model village' in the mid-nineteenth century by the then owner of the castle and estate, Louisa, Marchioness of Waterford. Lady Waterford had an avid interest in the welfare of

Ford Castle.

Ford Smithy.

her estate workers and rebuilt the village's housing stock to bring it up to date, adding a new school, which is now the village hall.

On-street car parking is available in the village and I found that the centre of the village was ideal for exploring its points of interest within a short walk.

The Grade I-listed castle is not open to the public but a permitted path does link it with the village and therefore the visitor is able to wander to the entrance at the portcullis gate to view the courtyard and main building. The Heron family acquired the property through marriage and in 1338 received permission from King Edward III to crenellate the building and set about enlarging and creating a more substantial building. Over the centuries the castle was subjected to attacks both from the Scots and from other Northumberland families such as the Manner family who owned nearby Etal Castle. During 1549 the castle was attacked by a French army of 6,000 troops, who under the leadership of General d'Esse were headed for Scotland to support the Scots in the Border Wars. A major change to the castle occurred in 1723 when, through marriage, it came into the ownership of the Delaval family. In the later part of the eighteenth century John Hussey Delaval demolished the building, replacing it with a Gothic mansion.

The castle and estate was purchased by James Joicey, 1st Baron Joicey, in 1907 and remains in the hands of the Joicey family, although the castle is currently leased as an outdoor education centre.

While the village has many interesting buildings, one did take my eye: the Grade II-listed former smithy at the east end of the main street, built as a blacksmith's shop in 1863 as part of the modernisation of the village by Lady Waterford. The horseshoe-shaped entrance certainly emphasises its original industrial purpose and in subsequent years it has been used as a house and is currently an antiques shop.

Another building associated with Lady Waterford is the Grade II*-listed former village school, now the village hall, known as Lady Waterford Hall. Dating from 1860, the interior contains a series of paintings in a Pre-Raphaelite style by the Marchioness of biblical scenes using local children and her employees as models. It took Lady Waterford twenty-one years to complete the artwork.

9. Norham

Norham is a small village that lies on the England–Scotland border and is easily reached from the A698 road, which runs between Berwick-upon-Tweed and Coldstream.

It was known in Saxon times as 'Ubbanford', meaning the fording place of Ubba. The name Norham is taken from the Middle English 'North Homestead'.

The village is dominated by the twelfth-century castle, which was built by Ranulf Flambard, Bishop of Durham in 1121. Ownership of Norham meant that the area was the northernmost enclave of the County Palatine of Durham, a county within a county, eventually being absorbed into Northumberland in 1844.

The castle stands on a rocky plateau above the River Tweed and was built to protect what was an important crossing point between England and Scotland. Due to its strategic position it was attacked on numerous occasions over a 450-year period and was described as the most dangerous place in England. For instance in 1318 Robert the Bruce and his Scottish army lay siege to the castle for a year without success. The castle fell out of use in the sixteenth century and turned into the ruin that it is today under the guardianship of English Heritage and is a Grade I-listed building and Scheduled Ancient Monument status. Entry is free, a small car park is provided and on-street parking is available in the village, which is a short distance from the castle. If using the car park entrance the castle grounds is via Sheeps Gate in the south curtain wall; the village entry is through the West Gate, also known as Marmions Gate.

Such was the romantic appeal of the castle that the eighteenth-century landscape artist Joseph Mallord William Turner painted it on a number of occasions, one of which, *Norham Castle, Sunrise*, hangs in the Tate Gallery, London.

The village is ranged around a triangular-shaped village green with a small number of shops and pubs. The Village Cross (Preaching Cross) dates from

Above: Norham Castle Keep from the West Gate.

Below: St Cuthbert's Church.

medieval times and is Grade II listed, the stepped base being original and the shaft dating from 1870.

Near the Village Green is the Grade I-listed St Cuthbert's Church, built in the twelfth century on the site of an earlier stone chapel dating from AD 830. Saint Cuthbert's body was brought to Norham in AD 875 when Lindisfarne Monastery was under threat from the Danes.

10. Percy's Cross

To the left-hand side of the A697 road, 3 miles north of the village of Powburn, is the Scheduled Ancient Monument and Grade II*-listed Percy's Cross, which was erected to commemorate the death of Sir Ralph Percy at the Battle of Hedgeley Moor on 23 April 1454.

Unfortunately there is no signposting, but the monument is located to the rear of a row of cottages and public access can be gained via a track leading through the wood to the immediate north (left) of the building's perimeter.

Sir Ralph was the son of the Earl of Northumberland, who, in the fifteenth century, sided with the House of Lancaster in the War of the Roses. The Battle of Hedgeley Moor was fought between the Yorkist force led by John Neville, 1st Marquis of Montague, and the Lancastrian army commanded by Henry

Percy's Cross.

Percy family emblem.

Beaufort, Duke of Somerset, with lieutenants, Sir Ralph Percy, Sir Ralph Grey, Lords Roos and Hungerford. The battle commenced with roughly equal forces of 5,000 men on each side. However during the conflict some 2,000 men under the banners of Lords Roos and Hungerford took flight and abandoned the battle fleeing to the south-west. Legend has it that Sir Ralph Percy was warned by a soothsayer the night before that this desertion would happen. As the battle raged the Yorkist's took the upper hand and many of the Lancastrian army left the field, leaving only Percy and his loyal household retainers to continue with the fight, but all were soon slain.

As a testimonial, Percy's Cross was erected sometime after the end of the War of the Roses (1485) by Ralph's nephew, Henry Percy, 4th Earl of Northumberland. The sandstone cross now consists only of the column, the head having disappeared over the centuries. The railings were a nineteenth-century addition. The 3-metre (10-foot) column bears relief carvings of the Percy Crescent and other family emblems.

The site of the battle itself is a few hundred metres from the site of the cross. Drive north on the A697 road and on the left-hand side, opposite a woodyard, is a lay-by. Parking there, you can enter a dedicated viewing area that has information boards setting out the course of the conflict.

11. Ratcheugh Crag

Located between Alnwick and Longhoughton is the Grade I-listed Ratcheugh Observatory, owned by the Duke of Northumberland and not generally open to the public. It is however open from time to time when the duke allows charities to hold open days – my visit was made on such an occasion.

On the heights of Ratcheugh Crag, it was commissioned by Hugh Percy, 1st Duke of Northumberland, so that he and his wife could gaze out over the surrounding countryside and coastal belt on their regular coach-driven rides around their Northumberland estate.

The folly was designed by the Scottish architect Robert Adam (1728–92) and built by John Bell of Durham sometime around 1754. The cottage was added by the 2nd Duke of Northumberland in 1880 and is still a private residence. It has a castellated Gothic style, with two semicircular turrets either side of a square central tower containing the viewing platform in the upper level. The design gives the impression of a ruined castle when viewed at a distance.

The observatory in its high position allows for a panoramic 360-degree view over Northumberland, covering inland to Alnwick, The Cheviot Hills and the North Sea Coastal Strip. It isn't difficult to imagine the duke looking out at all that he could behold and which he owned.

Ratcheugh Observatory.

Looking east to the coast.

12. Union Bridge

The Grade I-listed Union Suspension Bridge crosses the River Tweed linking England and Scotland between the villages of Horncliffe and Fishburn. It can be reached from the A698 road, which runs between Berwick-upon-Tweed and Coldstream.

Union Bridge from the west.

Standing on Union Bridge.

The first suspension bridge to be built in Britain and today, it is the oldest still in use worldwide. It was built between 1819 and 1820 by Berwick and North Durham Turnpike Trust. It originally carried a toll charge but is now free to pass by car or on foot. Captain Samuel Brown RN used his expertise in the production and use of ships' anchor cables to design the wrought-iron chains that support the wooden roadway.

The bridge is 112 metres (368 feet) long, 5.5 metres (18 feet) wide and is 8 metres (27 feet) above the river. On the Scottish side the bridge is supported on a pier of pink sandstone with the English side being built into a cliff. Both the pier and cliff bear a plaque of intertwined roses and thistles with the inscription 'Vis Units Forties 1820', translated as 'United Strength is Stronger'.

13. Wallington

Wallington Hall is signposted from the A696 road, turning off onto the B6342 road, and is also accessible from Morpeth on the B6343 road.

The name Wallington is Old English meaning 'farmstead of Wealth's people'.

The National Trust are guardians of the Grade I-listed hall and it is open to the public – the house is accessible between March and the end of October.

A Pele Tower was built on the site by the Fenwick family in 1475, but suffering from financial difficulties they sold the property and estate to Sir William Blackett in 1689. The Blackett family were Newcastle upon Tyne-based wealthy merchants with extensive commercial interests including coal mining and shipping. At the time they owned the largest house in Newcastle, which was based in its own large grounds at Anderson Place. It is thought that Sir William purchased the Pele as a country retreat, 32 kilometres (20 miles) from Newcastle, and may have used the building as a shooting lodge. In 1688 the Pele Tower was demolished and construction of the present hall commenced. It is interesting that the ground floor of the original building was retained as the cellars of the hall. Further modifications were made in 1745 when Sir Walter Calverley Blackett was left the estate in the will of Sir Walter. Those alterations were designed to a Palladian style by the architect Daniel Garrett. Between the years 1853 and 1854 Newcastle architect John Dobson designed further changes to the hall including the addition of a roof to the central quadrangle courtyard to form the Central Hall.

The Trevelyan family came into ownership of the Wallington estate in 1777 and held it until 1941 when Sir Charles Phillips Trevelyan donated it to the State.

A short walk from the car park you enter the grounds of the hall though the archway of the Clock Tower Gate, passing into the courtyard. The buildings in the Clock Tower formed the stables and are now operated as a café and shop. Passing through the courtyard you enter the hall, which was extensively internally restored by the Trevelyan family in 1928 with further works by the

Wallington Hall viewed from the south.

Dragon heads.

National Trust in the 1960s. The hall's many rooms, all tastefully decorated and full of original furniture and fittings, are freely available to the visitor. My own favourite room is the Central Hall, which contains fine painting and sculptures. Several Pre-Raphaelite murals adorn the walls, painted by William Bell Scott.

The extensive gardens of the hall are open to the public and were laid out under the guidance of the landscape architect Lancelot 'Capability' Brown, who was born at nearby Kirkharle.

On the front lawn of the hall are a set of four sculptured dragon heads. The limestone heads are Grade II* listed and arrived in the port of Newcastle from London in 1760 as part of ballast on one of the Blackett's coal ships. They were originally located at Rothley Castle, a folly on the Wallington estate, and were relocated to their present position in 1928. It is thought that the heads date from the sixteenth century and as gargoyles would have adorned a building in London.

South East

14. Blyth

The town of Blyth is located on the south-east coast of Northumberland, 21 kilometres (13 miles) to the north-east of Newcastle upon Tyne.

Lying at the mouth of the River Blyth, the town has maritime roots and still operates as a busy seaport.

The name Blyth is derived from the Old English 'Blida', meaning 'gentle' or 'merry', and at different stages in its development has been known as 'Blithmuth' and 'Blithermuth'.

The earliest recorded occupation is in the twelfth century when salt pans were built on a spit of land at the mouth of the river. This industry entailed the heating of brine to evaporate the seawater, leaving salt. It may well be that it was around this time that salt was exported by ship from the river.

Blyth became a major industrial area in the eighteenth century with the port exporting coal and grain; additionally it commenced shipbuilding, which was to continue until the 1960s. Among the long list of vessels built in Blyth was the first HMS *Ark Royal*, the Royal Navy's first seaplane carrier, constructed in 1914. The port has also been used in the past for shipbreaking with many vessels scrapped, ranging from passenger ships, Royal Naval ships and submarines of the German and Soviet Union navies.

The town centre of Blyth is dominated by the Market Square surrounded by a variety of shops including the indoor Keel Row Shopping Centre, which opened in the 1990s.

The quayside area of Blyth has undergone major redevelopment in the last decade, with heritage buildings such as the late eighteenth-century Custom House being converted into offices.

An interesting part of Blyth is Bath Terrace, which lies to the immediate south-east of the town centre. Many of the houses, which date from the late eighteenth century, are Grade II- listed and were originally occupied by Blyth's rich families, such as John Carr who owned several collieries. One in particular

Bath Terrace.

Former High Lights.

is worthy of mention, and that stands at No. 11. My eye was drawn to this building by the word 'Baths' inscribed on its porch. While built as a house in 1790 it was converted into a bathhouse during the early nineteenth century.

At that time it was fashionable for the upper classes to take cold baths as it was thought health benefits could be achieved. It is now a private home.

While on Bath Terrace it is hard to ignore the white tower that dominates from behind the roofline. Located at the rear of the terrace, this is the Grade II-listed High Light, a lighthouse built in 1788 and extended in both the eighteenth and twentieth centuries. The lighthouse acted as a navigational aid for vessels entering the port and was lit until 1985.

15. Bothal

Located south of the A197 road, 5 kilometres (3 miles) east of the town of Morpeth, is the small village of Bothal. 'Hidden' in a hollow next to the River Wansbeck, it features an ancient castle and church.

The name Bothal, pronounced locally as 'Bot-Hal', has two suggested meanings: either the Old English 'Botan Heale', meaning land by the river belonging to an Anglo-Saxon leader called Bota, or 'Botl', translated as a dwelling. It is recorded as 'Botthalle' in documents from 1233.

Entering Bothal the castle becomes visible on the right-hand side of the road, located at the bottom of a bank on a spur between the River Wansbeck and the Bothal Burn. The castle itself is private, but views can be achieved by looking over fields and the gatehouse from the village itself. The castle is both a Scheduled Ancient Monument and Grade I-listed building. Built on a

Bothal Castle from the west.

Ogle Altar Tomb.

natural mound, it may well have been an ancient defended village but came into prominence in 1343 when Sir Robert Bertram was granted permission from the King to crenellate (fortify) his mansion house. Fortifications were then added to the building including extensive curtain walls, large courtyard and gatehouse with portcullis. The castle fell out of use in the 1644 and was a ruin until the nineteenth century when steps were taken to modify and restore the gatehouse into living accommodation. These days the gatehouse is used as a private residence and commercial offices.

Standing close to the entrance to the castle is the Grade I-listed parish church of St Andrew. A church is thought to have been on the site since Anglo-Saxon times and there is evidence of a stone built building on the site in AD 875. The present Norman-style building was erected in the twelfth century with additions and modifications being made in the fourteenth century, extensive restoration being carried out in 1887. The church contains many historically interesting artefacts, among them the alabaster altar tomb of Ralph, 3rd Lord Ogle, and his wife, Margaret Gascoigne, dating from 1516.

Passing the church and adjacent to the castle entrance, a small unpaved lane leads down to the River Wansbeck where a series of stepping stones cross the waterway. A suspension footbridge also passes over the river at this point but it isn't open for public use.

16. Cramlington

Located close to Cramlington and signposted from the A1068 road is Northumberlandia, the Lady of the North, a human form sculpture of a reclining lady. The site is also accessible by bus services from Newcastle upon Tyne.

Car parking is available at the entrance, which also hosts a visitor centre and café. Entry to the park is free but donations are welcomed.

In 46 acres of parkland, the sculpture rises to 30 metres (100 feet) and has 6.5 kilometres (4 miles) of footpaths that climb its structure and provide a walk around its lakes. Formed from 1.5 million tons of waste clay, soil and rocks taken from the adjacent Shotton surface coal mine and costing £3 million, it was funded by Banks Group and the Blagdon estate. Designed by American-born architect and artist Charles Jencks, the sculpture was officially opened by HRH The Princess Royal on 3 September 2012.

Views from the higher parts of the sculpture give magnificent views in all directions, taking in the Cheviot Hills, North Sea and the conurbation of Tyneside. Additionally an industrial view can be achieved as the site overlooks the ongoing extraction of coal and fireclay at Shotton Mine.

While the majority of the pathways are gently inclined, there are some that are quite steep – but these are well signposted. I found the walkways to be easily accessible and well worth the effort to take in the views. An additional feature is a woodland trail which has numerous information.

Right: Northumberlandia looking east.

Below: Northumberlandia head and torso.

17. Matfen

The picturesque village of Matfen is located 20 miles west of Newcastle upon Tyne and 5 miles north of Corbridge and is best reached via the B6318 road.

The name Matfen is from the Old English 'Matta's fen', Matta being the name of a person who owned an area of low-lying marshland.

The village was purpose built in the nineteenth century to house workers on the Matfen Estate and at Matfen Hall, both owned the Blackett family. Ranged around a village green are a number of Grade II-listed buildings that are worthy of inspection, including Blackett House (a former temperance hotel) Church of Holy Trinity and a drinking fountain dating from 1886.

An interesting feature of the village green is that it is bisected by a watercourse that feeds the Whittle Dene Reservoir; consequently four bridges enable traffic and pedestrians to pass over the stream.

On the approach to the village from the B6318 turnoff and located on the right-hand side of the road is the Matfen Standing Stone, also known as the Stob Stone, a Prehistoric sandstone monolith (menhir). A Scheduled Ancient Monument and Grade II listed, the stone stands at a height of 2.7 metres (9 feet). Not immediately noticeable, the stone contains numerous prehistoric man-made cup marks on its lower faces. The meaning of such marks has been lost over time,

Matfen Village Green.

The Stob Stone.

but some consider them to be an art form and others a more practical purpose connected with grinding. It is not thought to be in its original position, having been located by farmers during ploughing and subsequently relocated to the present site.

Opposite is the architecturally interesting farmhouse known as the Standing Stone, now operating as a bed and breakfast establishment. Grade II-listed, it dates from 1700 and has an eighteenth-century castellated parapet and cruciform slit modification giving a Gothic look to the building.

18. Mitford

The small village of Mitford is located 3 kilometres (1.8 miles) west of Morpeth on the B6343 road.

The name Mitford is Old English for 'myth ford', meaning 'between two fords'. The village lies between the rivers Font and Wansbeck and both would have been fording points in the past.

The village is dominated by Mitford Castle, a ruin since the fourteenth century, and is best observed from outside of St Mary Magdalene Church.

Above: The ruined Mitford Castle.

Left: St Mary Magdalene Church Tower.

On private land, it isn't open to the public. A motte-and-bailey castle was built on a rocky outcrop in 1135 by William Bertram, Baron of Mitford, and fortified in stone by his son Roger in 1166. By the fourteenth century the castle as a fortification was abandoned and fell into the ruin that we see today. The ruins consist mainly of the curtain walls and a gateway, but when it was an active castle it contained a five-sided keep, which is unique in England – usually they are four-sided. The castle is a Scheduled Ancient Monument and Grade I-listed building.

Opposite the castle is the Grade I-listed St Mary Magdalene Church, originally built in the twelfth century (around the same time as the castle) and replaced a Saxon church. There is evidence inside the church from the Norman period including pillars on the south side of the nave and also a bell which was cast in 1150 and is claimed to be the oldest in Great Britain. The church was in a ruinous state when, in 1840, it was reroofed and restored. It was much enlarged in 1870 to a design by Newcastle architect R. J. Johnson (1832–92). At the eastern edge of the churchyard is an interesting archway, used as gateway to the vicarage. The archway may have been a Norman arched window from the previous church.

19. Morpeth

The market town of Morpeth is located off the A1 road, 26 kilometres (16 miles) north of Newcastle upon Tyne. The town has a railway station linked to the main east coast railway line.

Car parking in the town is free but some car parks require the use of a parking disc, which can be purchased from local shops.

The name Morpeth is said to be derived from the Old English for 'murder path', although there are no details to explain what crime may have been committed. Records dating from 1200 show the place name as 'Morpath' and another explanation for the meaning could be a 'path across a moor'.

Early records show that William de Merley was awarded the Barony of Morpeth in 1095 and he built a motte-and-bailey castle overlooking the ford crossing the River Wansbeck. That castle was destroyed in the twelfth century by King John of England as retribution against the de Merley family, who had sided with his enemy, King Alexander II of Scotland. The mound on which the castle was built can still be seen in Carlisle Park, which lies to the southern bank of the River Wansbeck. The mound is now known as Haa' Hill (Haw Hill).

A second stone castle was built to the south of its predecessor in the fourteenth century by William de Greystoke. The gatehouse of the castle and a section of its curtain wall are all that remain today and are both a Scheduled Ancient Monument and Grade I-listed building. The castle was all but ruined by a siege by Scottish forces in 1644 when it was besieged for twenty-six days and pounded

Above: Morpeth Castle Gatehouse.

Left: Morpeth Clock Tower from Market Place.

with some 200 cannonballs. The gatehouse was restored by the Landmark Trust in 1990 and is now a boutique holiday let.

Located in the Market Place is the Grade II-listed free-standing Clock Tower, dating from the seventeenth century and made from stone recycled from the nearby Newminster Abbey, which was closed during the Reformation. Originally two storeys, the third floor was added to the 21-metre- (70-foot-) high tower in 1705 to house six bells donated by the town's Member of Parliament, Major General Edmund Maine. The bells chimed at eight o'clock each evening to mark the end of the day and to tell residents to 'deaden their fires and retire for the evening' in readiness for work the next morning.

20. Newbiggin-by-the-Sea

The small town of Newbiggin-by-the-Sea is located in south-east Northumberland, 3 kilometres (1.86 miles) west of Ashington. A seaside resort, there is adequate parking throughout the town but the major car park can be located to the north-east next to Newbiggin Maritime Centre.

The name is from the Old English 'Niwe Biggin', meaning 'new house or building'.

Located in a natural bay, it was historically used as a seaport from as early as the fourteenth century when grain and coal were exported by sailing ships. It is

The *Couple Sanding* art installation.

St Bartholomew's Church.

now home to a handful of commercial traditional Northumbrian fishing cobles, but in 1869 it was recorded that 142 boats were based in Newbiggin.

A holiday destination since the early 1800s, the town went through a major redevelopment of its tourist facilities in 2007 involving the replenishment of its beach with 500,000 tons of sand delivered by sea from Skegness. At the same time a breakwater to protect the beach from erosion was built and included Britain's first permanent offshore sculpture, *The Couple*. Standing 274 metres (300 yards) from the beach, at a height of 12.5 metres (41 feet), the sculpture by Sean Henry features a pair of 5-metre (16.4-feet) painted bronze figures gazing out to sea. To complement the sculpture two life-size replicas of the figures can be seen on the promenade towards the lifeboat station.

The town is dominated by St Bartholomew's Church, which is located on a headland (Church Point) on the northern side of the bay. The landmark church and its spire can be seen up and down the north-east coast and have been used by sailors as a navigational beacon for many centuries. It is thought that the monks of Lindisfarne may have built a chapel on the promontory as early as the ninth century, but the stone building has its roots in the thirteenth century when it was built as a chapel of ease for nearby Woodhorn. The church was in a ruinous state when, in 1845, a decision was taken to restore the building. The church was damaged in both world wars: on 19 March 1921 a sea mine that had been washed ashore was in the process of being deactivated when it exploded, causing extensive damage to the church; in the Second World War, a parachute mine exploded close to the building on 15 February 1941 causing damage to the church.

21. Ponteland

The village of Ponteland is located 12.1 kilometres (7.5 miles) north-west of Newcastle upon Tyne on the A696 road. There are a number of shops, cafes and public houses in the village; free parking is available in a number of municipal car parks.

The name is derived from the Old English meaning 'island in the Pont' – the River Pont runs through the village and the name Pont is an Old Celtic word for 'pant', meaning valley.

The Grade I-listed Church of St Mary the Virgin dates from the twelfth century with additions made in the period to the fifteenth century. Restorations were carried out during the nineteenth century including changes to the roof and alterations to the height of the internal floors. The Norman tower was part of the twelfth-century building with an additional level (bell stage) being added in the fourteenth century. The church is usually open to the public during the day and is well worth a visit. The churchyard contains several Grade II-listed headstones and tombs including the resting place of Sir Charles Ogle, Bart, Admiral of the Fleet.

In front of the church is Coates Green, named after the Coates School, which stood on the land until it was demolished in 1968. *The Teaching* sculpture by David Edwick was commissioned by Ponteland Parish Council in 2001 as a Millennium project. Featuring a teacher and children, it is made from Ulverston marble.

Coates Green and Church of St Mary the Virgin.

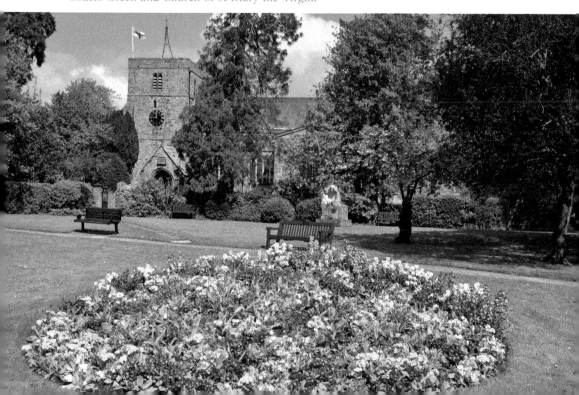

The Blackbird Inn.

To the west of the church is The Blackbird Inn, a Grade II*-listed former manor house but now a public house and restaurant. Originally the site of Ponteland Castle, it is historically important as the place where King Henry VIII and King Alexander of Scotland met to sign a peace treaty in 1236. Unfortunately the castle was destroyed by the Earl of Douglas and his Scottish army in 1388. In 1597 the ruined and abandoned castle was acquired by Mark Errington, who built a manor house in its place, incorporating some parts of the castle, including a medieval tower.

Also worth a visit is the sixteenth-century Grade II-listed Vicar's Pele Tower, which stands to the north side of Main Street. Originally built to house and protect the vicars of Ponteland from attacks, it was restored in 1971.

22. Seaton Delaval

The country house Seaton Delaval Hall is 15 kilometres (9 miles) north-west of Newcastle upon Tyne and is reached via the A190 road running between Seaton Sluice and Seaton Delaval village.

Seaton Delaval as a place name is based on two factors: the Seaton Burn, which runs through the area to the North Sea, and de la Val being the family name of the Norman French followers granted lands by William the Conqueror.

Travelling along The Avenue (A190) it is impossible to miss the grandeur of the western elevation and courtyard of the hall. Turning through the main gates the car park and entry point to the site is well signposted to the right-hand side. The hall and its gardens are under the guardianship of the National Trust and an admission charge is payable.

The Grade I-listed hall was designed by the English architect and playwright Sir John Vanbrugh in an English baroque style and replaced an earlier Tudor period mansion. This is claimed to be Vanbrugh's finest work and it was the last building to be designed by the architect. Built for Admiral George Delaval, the works took from 1718 to 1728 to complete – unfortunately George was killed in 1723 when he fell from his horse and never viewed the completed hall. Vanbrugh died in 1726 and likewise did not live long enough to see his completed design.

A major fire in 1822 caused major damage to the central block of the building when its floors, contents and roof were gutted. Fortunately the east and west wings were saved from fire damage. Work was carried out between 1859 and 1860 under the direction of Newcastle architect John Dobson to strengthen the building and to replace its roof. Further restorations were carried out in the 1950s when Sir Edward Delaval Henry Astley, Lord Hastings, acquired the property. In 2008 guardianship was taken over by the National Trust and a program of restoration put into place (which still continues), a £3.7 million restoration grant having been awarded by the National Lottery Heritage Fund in April 2018.

The hall and its gardens are a pleasure to explore and I found the purchase of a guidebook from the site shop to be a great help to understand and navigate the different parts of the building. Numerous National Trust volunteers are available on-site if you do need to ask a question or directions.

Seaton Delaval Hall front elevation.

Seaton Delaval Hall rear elevation.

The delight of Seaton Delaval Hall is that you are free to wander its rooms, whether that is the Entrance Hall with its chequerboard marble floor, ornate fireplace and its arcade's holding sculptured figures or the Saloon with its walls stripped back to the original stone with strengthening columns installed during the Dobson restoration.

The East Wing was the original stables and coach house, and many of its original fittings remain including the name plates of horses.

The West Wing was originally the domestic staff accommodation but was later to be used as apartments for the owners after the fire of 1822. It is now well appointed with furniture, paintings, sculptures and other historical artefacts.

23. Seaton Sluice

Located on the A193 road between Whitley Bay and Blyth is the small coastal village of Seaton Sluice, which originally grew up around a small natural harbour.

Now a 'commuter town', it is home to some 3,000 residents and is well served by five public houses, a social club as well as local shops and cafes.

Above: Seaton Sluice Harbour.

Below: The Octagon.

It was originally known as Hartley Pans, which recognised the fact that the major industry was the production of salt by the evaporation of seawater. Its name changed to Seaton Sluice in the eighteenth century when a canal lock, known locally as 'The Cut', was built, creating another channel from the North Sea to the port. Seaton Burn is the name of the river on which the village stands; 'sluice' was the water gate mechanism used to fill and empty the lock. The harbour was improved by the local landowner John Hussey Delaval in 1761 when a decision was taken to cut a canal lock linking the harbour to the sea, allowing larger sailing ships to use the port. A channel was cut through rock to a length of 274 metres (900 feet) and on 22 March 1768 was first used by the sailing ship *Warkworth* to load coal destined for London. The port was subsequently used to export locally produced glass and copperas but fell out of use on 20 May 1872 when the last ship, Unity, sailed with a cargo of glass bottles for the Channel Islands.

These days the harbour is home to a range of commercial fishing and pleasure boats but much of its history as a working port can still be seen, the most noticeable being the now empty and unused lock. Located beside The Kings Arms public house, the winding mechanism for raising and lowering the water gate has been preserved. A pleasant walk to the locally known 'Rocky Island' is accessed from this point crossing a wooden footbridge. The island contains the historic Watch Tower, now used as a museum, which was built in 1880 for the Seaton Sluice Life Saving Co.

Another maritime reminder is the Grade II-listed 'Octagon', which stands next to the Waterford Arms public house. Dating from 1750, it was built as the Harbour Office and is thought to have been designed by Sir John Vanbrugh. Now an art gallery, it was also used in past years as a private residence.

24. Warkworth

The ancient village of Warkworth lies 9.5 kilometres (6 miles) south-east of the town of Alnwick and is best reached via the A1068 road. Car parking is available in the Market Place and also The Stanners, both of which are signposted.

The village is a popular tourist location and consequently caters for the visitor with a number of shops, café's, hotels and public houses. Many of the historical points of interest are accessible within a short walk of the Market Place but the castle does stand at the top of a fairly steep hill. It does however have its own car park for easier access.

The earliest record of the village is AD 737 when King Ceolwulf of Northumbria granted the church and village of Werceworde to the Monastery of Lindisfarne. The meaning of Werceworde is 'homestead of Werce', and it is claimed Werce was an Abbess. It may well be that the village had a nunnery.

On a spur of the River Coquet, the village is located in an ideal defensive position and in 1157 Henry II granted permission for Roger fitz Richard to erect a motte-and-bailey castle on the hill overlooking the village. Unfortunately the defences of that wooden-built castle were considered to be poor and when Duncan, Earl of Fife, launched a Scottish raid in 1174, the local inhabitants chose to seek sanctuary in the stone-built church of St Lawrence. However the result of that decision was the slaughter of 300 souls within the church.

Over the centuries Warkworth Castle was transformed into a formidable stone-built fortification dominating and giving protection to the village. These days the Grade I-listed building is under the guardianship of English Heritage and open to the public. Much of the castle was built by the Percy family but it was neglected between the seventeenth and eighteenth centuries. Thankfully the 4th Duke of Northumberland, Algernon Percy, decided to restore the castle in 1850. There are information boards in the grounds and buildings of the castle, which are comprehensive, but I found it helpful to purchase a guidebook from the site shop.

The Grade I-listed Church of St Lawrence is well worth a visit and is usually open to the public throughout the day. As indicated above, a church was

Warkworth Castle.

View looking over Warkworth village.

mentioned in records from Anglo-Saxon times but the present building dates from the Norman period, dating from 1132 to 1140 with alterations and additions being added in subsequent centuries. In 1860 it was reported that the building was in a 'ruinous condition' and major restoration was undertaken including the replacement of the nave roof.

South West

25. Bellingham

On the route of the B6320 road, lying beside the River North Tyne, is the market town of Bellingham, pronounced 'Bell in jum'. The town takes its name from the De Bellingham family who owned lands in the area.

While this is a comparatively small town, it is a popular stopping point for tourists and also a staging point for those partaking in the Pennine Way National Trail. It also has numerous historical features all within walking distance of the town centre, two of which are described below.

The Grade II-listed St Cuthbert's Well, known locally as Cuddy's Well, is located to the south of St Cuthbert's Church and is thought to have miraculous properties. It is claimed the spring was discovered by St Cuthbert while dowsing and subsequently blessed by him. Its waters, which never dry up, are still used in the Church of St Cuthbert for baptisms.

Reginald of Durham, writing in the middle of the twelfth century, reports a miracle involving a young girl called Edda who, despite it being the Holy Day of St Lawrence, insisted on sewing a dress. As a consequence of this act her left hand contracted in such a way that she couldn't release the cloth that she was working with. She was taken to St Cuthbert's Well, where she drank the water and then spent the night within the church. At dawn she woke and witnessed a vision of St Cuthbert, who touched her hand and she was able to release the cloth. However she screamed and caused the apparition to disappear and her hand again contracted. Masses were then said on nine successive days involving a novena (devotional prayers repeated for nine days or weeks) by the local congregation and this brought about her recovery and she regained use of her hand.

The well was surrounded by a structure in the eighteenth century, known locally as a pant, and the cover is thought to be medieval in origin.

An interesting historical artefact on display, located between Manchester Square and High Street, Bellingham, Northumberland, is a Chinese gingall. A Chinese gingall is a light canon and this particular one was captured during

St Cuthbert's Well.

The Chinese Gingall.

the Boxer Rebellion from the Taku Forts in China. Admiral Sir Edward Charlton, then a commander on the Royal Naval Cruiser HMS *Orlando*, took part in the action in June 1900 and the gingall fell into his 'guardianship'. Edward Charlton was related to the Charlton family, whose ancestral home was the nearby Hesleyside Hall. He donated the trophy to the town in 1902.

26. Brinkburn Abbey

A Scheduled Ancient Monument, Grade I-listed Brinkburn Abbey is signposted from the A697 Morpeth to Wooler road, turning off onto the B6334 road; the site is on the left.

English Heritage operates the site and it is open to the public between April and October excepting Mondays and Tuesdays. A free car park is provided some 400 metres (1312 feet) from the entrance.

Founded by William de Bertram, 1st Baron Mitford, in the twelfth century for Black Canons of the Augustine Order, the abbey was built between 1130 and 1135 by the Master Mason Osbert Colutarius. The site for the abbey was well chosen, being in a secluded and peaceful spot at the base of a ravine on a loop in the Ricer Coquet. The abbey fell into ruin after the Dissolution of the Monasteries in the sixteenth century but was rescued by the Cadogan family, who had acquired the abbey and its grounds in the nineteenth century. Newcastle-based architect Thomas Austin was commissioned to design a restoration of the building and works were undertaken between 1858 and 1859. As a consequence of the nineteenth-century restoration the building was much remodelled, but many of the original features can still be seen.

Brinkburn Abbey (right) and Manor House (left).

Adjacent to the abbey is the Grade II*-listed Manor House, built in the sixteenth century for the Fenwick family. The house incorporates parts of the southern area of the original abbey. In 1810 it was remodelled in a Gothic style and further extended by Newcastle architect John Dobson between 1830 and 1837. While the building is undergoing restoration, the ground floor and basement of the building were open to the public at the time of writing.

One story about the abbey goes back to the times of the Scots Raiders when it was a regular occasion for Northumberland to be attacked from the north. On one occasion the attackers became lost in nearby woodland and being unable to locate the abbey, commenced their return home. Rejoicing at the turn of events the monks rang the abbey's bell with the unfortunate consequence of alerting the raiders to their location. It is claimed that following the attack the bell was thrown into the River Coquet, an area now known as the Bell Pool.

27. Chillingham

The Grade I-listed castle and church at Chillingham are easily reached via either the A1 or A697 roads, 47 miles north of Newcastle upon Tyne. The castle is well signposted from both roads.

The meaning of Chillingham comes from the Old English meaning 'homestead of Ceofel's people'.

The castle is open to the public between the end of March until the close of October and there is an admission charge. Its owners brand it as 'Britain's most haunted historic castle' and it has featured in many supernatural-type television programs.

Standing on high ground above the Chillingam Burn (stream), it was originally a manor house, and converted into a fortification in 1344 when the then owner, Thomas de Heton, received a licence to crenellate his building. The castle

Above: Chillingham Castle rear elevation.

Right: Grey Altar Tomb.

changed hands over the centuries but it eventually came into the ownership of the Earls of Tankerville. In 1936 the contents of the castle were auctioned and it was abandoned as a residence. By 1982 the building was in a ruinous state of repair when it was purchased by the present owner, Sir Humphrey Wakefield, who embarked upon a restoration project that has brought the castle and its gardens back to life. The castle is quadrilateral in shape, with towers at each corner linked by ranges of buildings and a central courtyard. Numerous rooms are accessible, most of which have been restored to their original purpose and contain many interesting historical objects. Not to be missed is the dungeon and the torture chamber containing instruments and apparatus used to extract information from captured prisoners.

The gardens, which were laid out by Sir Jeffrey Wyatville in 1828, are also open to the public.

The Grade I-listed Church of St Peter is a short walk from the castle and is usually open for public access. A delightful building sitting at the top of a small hill, it originates from the twelfth century with modifications and additions having been made in the subsequent centuries. Internally it contains many interesting features, perhaps the most notable being the altar tomb of Sir Ralph Grey and his wife, Elizabeth, located in the south chapel and dating from 1443. The alabaster figures of the Greys lie on the tomb with pet dogs at their feet. The tomb is made from sandstone and contains many sculptured religious figures and armorial symbols.

28. Chipchase Castle

Chipchase Castle is best reached from the B6320 road that runs from Chollerford to Wark, then follow the brown signposts.

The Anglo-Saxon village of Chipchase has long since been lost, but Chipchase Castle remains and lies on a plateau above the River North Tyne.

The name Chipchase is thought to be derived from the Old English word for 'cheap or market'.

A Grade I-listed building and Scheduled Ancient Monument, the castle is a private residence but is opened to the public in June of each year, a small charge being made. Originally built as a 15-metre (50-foot) defensive pele tower in the

Chipchase Castle front elevation.

Chipchase Castle Chapel.

fourteenth century by the Heron family, it was later to be extended and modified with the addition of a Jacobean mansion and later works in the Georgian and Victorian periods. The tower is clearly visible and can be seen at the left-hand side of the building. The Jacobean mansion was built in 1671 when the property was under the ownership of the Heron family. Internally the house contains many original features but is primarily a private residence and has a 'lived in' feeling rather than that of a museum, although many pieces are historic. It is worth mentioning that internal photography is not permitted.

Also open in June is the small sandstone-built Chipchase Castle Chapel, which stands opposite the entrance to the house. Grade I listed, it was originally medieval in age and rebuilt in 1735 by the then castle owner John Reed. Internally it has whitewashed walls and contains eighteenth-century furniture and fittings including pews and pulpit. There are memorials to the Reed family including their burial vault. A fine stained-glass window by Arnold Robinson commemorates Captain Hugh Taylor of the Scots Guards who was killed in action during the First World War.

29. Codger Fort

Travelling on the B6342 road between Rothbury and Scots Gap, a strange castle-like structure appears on a rocky crag to the left-hand side of the road. This is Codger Fort, sometimes referred to as Cadger Fort. The site is accessible to the public and there is a small parking space on the eastern roadside. A short walk up a small hill reaches the building, which offers good views of the surrounding countryside on all sides.

Codger's Fort view from south.

Codger's Fort Turret.

Grade II listed, the fort has an interesting history and appears to have been originally built by Sir Walter Calverley Blackett as a gun battery holding six naval cannons to protect the road, then known as Salter's Way, from any northern invaders during the time of the Jacobite Risings in the early part of the eighteenth century. It isn't thought that the guns were fired in anger. Sometime around 1770 Sir Walter was developing his Rothley Estate into a deer park and commissioned Thomas Wright to design a romantic ruined castle as a decorative feature – what we now call a folly. This is the structure we see today.

30. Cragside

The Cragside Estate is located some 5 kilometres (3 miles) south of the B6341, accessed from the A697 Morpeth to Coldstream road, and is well signposted. The estate is under the guardianship of the National Trust and an entrance fee is charged.

Consisting of 911 acres of woodland, the estate has over seven million trees, shrubs and plants, all of which can be seen from the 40 miles of footpaths and walks. A 6-mile carriage drive encircles the grounds and allows the visitor to take in its scale and also stop at the numerous viewpoints. Built and developed by the industrialist and inventor William Armstrong, Baron Armstrong of Cragside (1810–1900), the house and grounds were acquired by the National Trust in 1977 and opened to the public in 1979.

Armstrong had spent his childhood holidays in nearby Rothbury and in 1862 bought a parcel of land to build a modest country retreat. However in 1869 he decided to make Cragside his permanent home, a contributing factor being that the railway had been linked to Rothbury in 1862 and Armstrong could easily commute to his W. G. Armstrong & Co. factory in Elswick, Newcastle upon Tyne. Employing the architect R. Norman Shaw, he designed a mansion that was later to be described as the 'Palace of a Modern Magician'. Using his technical ingenuity Armstrong powered his estate and house using hydroelectricity, building five lakes to provide the initial energy required in the process. This was

Cragside Mansion entranceway.

Cragside Mansion from the south.

to enable his house to be the first one in the world to be lit by electricity, his friend Sir Joseph Swan providing his newly invented filament light bulbs. It may well be a case that Armstrong employed his knowledge of powering machinery by electricity and also through hydraulic power to impress his customers, who were often entertained at the estate.

The centrepiece of the estate is the Tudor Revival-style mansion, which Armstrong used both as a home and as a place for entertaining his customers and friends. The house contains many of the original fittings and the visitor is permitted to freely wander through its rooms. One room that caught my eye was the Drawing Room designed especially for a royal visit in 1884. The centrepiece is the splendid Early Renaissance, classical-style, double-storey, polished, Italian marble chimney piece, designed by William Lethaby and sculptured by Farmer and Brindley.

31. Elsdon

The village of Elsdon lies to the north-east of Otterburn, just off the A696 road. Many of the points of interest, including the Pele Tower, Church of St Cuthbert, Pinfold and Mote Hill can be reached within a small walk from the village centre.

The name Elsdon is from the Old English 'Eli's valley'. Eli or Ella was claimed to have been a 'giant' who lived in a den and terrorised the surrounding area.

The earliest record of the village is in 1080 when a Norman motte-and-bailey castle (Motte Hill) was built and it became the administrative capital of the area known as Redesdale.

Elsdon has a large village green and to its south is the Grade II-listed, eighteenth-century, stone-built circular pinfold that was once used to hold stray animals.

St Cuthbert's Parish Church lies to the north of the village green and is Grade I listed. Standing on the site of an earlier Saxon church, the current building contains fabric dating from the twelfth century with additions from later centuries. Restoration was carried out during two periods in the nineteenth century. Open to the public, a tour around the exterior and interior are recommended.

To the north of the church is the Grade I-listed Elsdon Tower, a fortified building known as a Pele Tower and first recorded in 1415 as the residence of the rector of St Cuthbert's Church. There is however a theory that the building may have been converted from an earlier shooting lodge, erected and used by the Lords of Redesdale, who had castles at Prudhoe and Harbottle. Many similar buildings appear in Northumberland and act as a defence against raiders crossing the border from Scotland. Now a private residence, the building can be viewed from its driveway.

Motte Hills to the north-east of the village was the site of the Norman motte-and-bailey castle, constructed by Robert de Umfaville in 1080. The castle was built from wood and nothing of this has survived, but the man-made earthworks are visible and open to the public. A Scheduled Ancient Monument, it is considered to be the best example of a motte-and-bailey castle in Northumberland.

The Grade II-listed Winter's Gibbet, also known as Steng's Cross, stands 3 miles from the village on the minor road heading east from Elsdon heading towards Cambo. The gibbet takes its name from William Winter, who in 1792, with sisters Jane and Eleanor Clark, broke into the home of Margaret Crozier at Raw Pele Tower, Elsdon. Margaret Crozier, an aged lady, was robbed and

Elsdon Castle,
Motte Hills.

murdered by the trio. Rather than making an escape they remained in Elsdon and were consequently apprehended by the police. Following guilty verdicts all three were hanged at Westgate, Newcastle, with the bodies of the two sisters being given to the barber surgeons for dissection. To set an example the body of Winter was put inside a gibbet cage and taken for display at Elsdon. The present gibbet is a replica of the original and was erected in 1867. A wooden body was placed in the cage to represent Winter, but this was removed when the locals used it for target practice and also cut off pieces to cure toothache. In later years the body was replaced by a replica head hanging from the gibbet, but that was also the subject of vandalism and at one stage stolen. As a result the authorities have decided not to replace the head.

32. Great Tosson

The hamlet of Great Tosson is best reached from the town of Rothbury. Passing over the River Coquet to the south on the B6342 road, turn immediately to the right at the end of the bridge and follow the signposts for Great Tosson.

The name Tosson is from the Old English 'Tot-Stan', meaning 'lookout stone' – certainly the position of Great Tosson gives splendid views over the Coquet Valley, looking as far as the Cheviot Hills.

Originally consisting of a group of farm buildings and an inn located around Tosson Tower (a fortified house), the buildings are now mainly holiday accommodation.

The ruined tower dates from the fifteenth century and its earliest recorded mention is in 1517 when William Ogle exchanged it with Lord Ogle for Cocklaw Tower, Northumberland. Both a Scheduled Ancient Monument and

Above: Remains of
Tosson Tower.

Right: View across the
Coquet Valley.

Grade II*-listed building, the tower had most of its external facing stones recycled in the eighteenth century, leaving the exposed internal rubble infill. The walls of the building were 2 metres (6.5 feet) thick, and it was composed of three floors offering protection to its inhabitants from the various hostile attackers who roamed Northumberland, often coming over the border from Scotland. Only the level to the first floor survives.

A short distance through the village can be found the Tosson Limekilns, dating from 1888; they were designed by Alnwick architect George Reavell for Lord William Armstrong.

Restored by Northumberland National Park Authority, the site has a small car park and is free to enter.

33. Harbottle

Located in the Coquet Valley, the small village of Harbottle is accessed via the C68 road off the B6341 road, the junction being some 8 kilometres (5 miles) south of the town of Rothbury.

The meaning of Harbottle comes from the Old English 'dwellings for the hirelings' or 'of the army'.

The village is grouped along both sides of a central high street and is dominated by the ruins of Harbottle Castle standing on a hill to the western edge. Thankfully for a small rural village it still boasts a pub, the Star Inn.

The village has two castles, details of which are explained below.

The oldest Harbottle Castle is accessed via a car park at the western end of the village. From the car park there is a short walk up a gently sloping hill to reach the remains of the Scheduled Ancient Monument and Grade I-listed building. While classified as a 'ruin', there are still parts of the castle to view, being a section of the curtain wall and the remains of the tower. The hill also offers good views of the village and surrounding countryside including the Cheviot Hills. Originally a motte-and-bailey castle built by the Umfraville family in 1151, it

Harbottle Castle ruins.

Clennell Memorial
Fountain.

was replaced by a stone fortification in the thirteenth century following attacks
by Border Raiders. In 1296 the castle withheld a siege by Robert the Bruce and
his army of 40,000. It wasn't so lucky in 1318 when Bruce and his Scottish army
returned and captured the castle. It is recorded that the castle was abandoned in
1715 and gradually became the ruin that it is today.

A new 'castle' was erected in the seventeenth century at the eastern end of the
village using stone recycled from the ruined castle. While it took the name of a
castle it was in reality a mansion house. However that building was replaced in
1829 when Newcastle architect John Dobson designed a new house for Fenwick
Clennell. The building is Grade II listed.

The Clennell family are commemorated with a Grade II-listed water fountain
which stands in the middle of the village. In memory of Harriet Pennell Clennell,
she must have been highly thought of to be immortalised by the inhabitants of
Harbottle. Designed by D. McMilan, the fountain was erected in 1880 and is
made from sandstone and polished granite. The cost of £120 was met from
public subscription. The inscription on the fountain reads: 'Mrs Clennell of
Harbottle Castle, died Nov 17th 1879, she devoted the powers of an active
mind, the impulses of a generous heart, and the industry of a busy life to the
welfare and happiness of the inhabitants of Harbottle and the neighbourhood.
To perpetuate her name and virtues they erected this fountain August 1880.'

34. Holystone

Directions to reach Holystone are as above for Harbottle. There is no car park
in the village and therefore considerate on street parking is required.

The name Holystone has a straightforward meaning; it relates to a stone with
a religious or saintly connection and may be associated with the twelfth-century
priory of Augustine Canonesses, which existed until its demolition in 1541.

To the north-west of the village, a quarter of a mile along a signposted path the Grade I-listed the Lady's Well nestles among an idyllic grove of trees. Under the guardianship of the National Trust the well is open to the public. The well has been known by a number of names: at one time it was known as the Well of St Paulinus and later as St Ninian's Well. However, it is now more commonly known as the Lady's Well, taking its name from the nuns of the Augustine priory – who dedicated it to the Virgin Mary. The association with Paulinus is from a mistake in a translation of the writing of the Venerable Bede, as it was originally thought that King Edwin and three thousands of his followers were baptised here on Easter Sunday AD 627 but later investigations showed that had occurred in York. Ninian, known as the Apostle of the Borders, was associated with the well in the fifth century. A roadway between Redesdale and the Devil's Causeway was built by the Roman's during their occupation and it is thought that the well

The Lady's Well and statue of Paulinus.

St Mary's Church.

not only became a watering place on the route but also a shrine. It may well be that the Roman's built the paved water tank that forms the pool. The statue of Paulinus once stood in the middle of the pool and was installed in 1780 when it was relocated from Alnwick Castle. It was replaced by the present cross in the nineteenth century. The well is fed from a spring and at one time was the water supply to the nearby village until in 1998 when mains water was installed.

In the village the visitor is recommended to visit the Grade II-listed St Mary's Church. Dating from the twelfth century, it was rebuilt between 1848 and 1849. The churchyard holds the grave of Newcastle architect Frank West Rich (1840–1929), who owned the nearby Dunes Hill Grange.

35. Kielder

Kielder Village lies 5 kilometres (3 miles) from the Scottish Border in the north-west of Northumberland and is best known for its large man-made forest and reservoir. If travelling from the south on the B6320 road, follow the brown signed route on the C200 road from Bellingham.

The village name is taken from the Kielder Burn, which runs through the village. 'Burn' is a North East England and Scottish term for a watercourse with a size between a stream and a small river.

The village is comprised of some sixty houses that were predominately built for forest workers in the 1950s. It does, however, have a Grade II-listed nineteenth-century United Reform Church and an eighteenth-century 'castle'.

Kielder Castle isn't a defensive building as the name suggests, but a folly built by the Duke of Northumberland as a castellated shooting box. It was erected as a base from which his shooting parties could hunt grouse on his surrounding moors. The architect for the building was Newcastle upon Tyne-based William Newton (1730–98). The castle is Grade II-listed and is now used as a visitor centre, small museum and café.

In 1932 the state obtained the Kielder estate as payment in lieu of death duties arising from the death of the then Duke of Northumberland. The Forestry Commission was tasked with developing a forest and built a model village at Kielder to house forestry workers, and the largest man-made forest in northern Europe was planted. Now covering 674 square kilometres (250 square miles), it remains the largest working forest in England.

Kielder Water Reservoir was opened by Her Majesty the Queen on 26 May 1982 and was at the time the largest man-made lake in northern Europe. Costing £167 million, it was constructed by Northumbrian Water to provide a water supply to the North East of England. It took four and a half years to complete

Above: Entrance to Kielder Castle.

Below: View looking over the reservoir.

and resulted in the loss of twenty-six family homes as well as farms and a school when the valley was flooded. With a capacity of 200 billion litres (44 billion gallons) of water, it has a shoreline measuring 43 kilometres (27 miles), a length of 11 kilometres (7 miles), and at its deepest point it is 52 metres (170 feet). Now a popular tourist attraction, many sporting and educational activities take place both on its waters and shores. One of those attractions is Kielder Observatory, which allows stargazers to view the night sky. Kielder is designated by the International Dark Sky Association as an International Dark Sky Park and has been awarded Gold Tier status for the high quality and lack of light pollution of the night sky. It is the largest Dark Sky Park area of protected night sky in Europe.

36. Lordenshaws Hill Fort

The car park for Lordenshaws Hill Fort lies on a minor road off the B6342 road, 6.4 kilometres (4 miles) south of the town of Rothbury. A brown signpost for Simonside indicates the turning to the right-hand side of the road.

From the free car park there is a marked pathway to the fort, which is located at a height of 264 metres (866 feet); the short walk is up a gentle slope.

Above: Iron Age hut circle remains.

Right: Prehistoric rock art.

The Iron Age fort is considered to date from at least 350 BC and was one of many fortified hill forts in Northumberland. Built on the top of a hill, it commands a panoramic view over the Coquet Valley, across to the Cheviot Hills and on a clear day to the North Sea. Roughly oval shaped, it was encircled by three ramparts with deep ditches between each of the two outer defences. The ramparts and ditches are easily identified. The fort had two entrances and these are marked by the pathway that passes through the main living area. Evidence of seven hut circles can be located within the site; small quantities of stones used in their build remain at foundation level.

Scattered around the boundary of the fort are a number of examples of Prehistoric rock art, taking the form of cups and rings carved into various rocky outcrops. Predating the hill fort there is no definitive explanation as to what the markings mean. Other numerous examples of such rock art can be found throughout Northumberland.

37. Rothbury

Located beside the River Coquet, the market town of Rothbury is often referred to as the 'Capital of Coquetdale'. Accessible via the B6344 and B6341 roads, which both run from the A697 Morpeth to Coldstream road, there is also an hourly bus service linking the town with Newcastle upon Tyne.

Armstrong Cross.

Village view.

While there is on-street car parking it is recommended that the free car park on the south side of the River Coquet is used, which is well signposted.

The meaning of Rothbury is from the Old English 'Routhebina', meaning 'Routha's settlement'. The earliest recorded mention is in 1090 when Henry I granted land to the monks of Tynemouth Priory to build a chapel. Its position on the River Coquet is likely the reason for a settlement here as the river was shallow allowing a ford crossing; a bridge was to be later built in 1461. There is a crossroads of routes running east to west and north to south, and the drovers road running from Alnmouth to Hexham passed through Rothbury. A market town, a charter to hold a cattle and wool sales was granted in 1291, although a market is no longer held in the town. Nowadays the town is very much a visitor destination with a range of pubs, cafés, shops and hotels. With the Simonside Hills to the south and Cheviots to the west, Rothbury makes an ideal location for tourists to either use the town as a base or as a stopping off point.

A walk up the long wide front street is highly recommended to view the many different buildings, mainly sandstone faced and dating from the eighteenth and nineteenth centuries. I found it a pleasant walk up one side of the road and back on the other, ending up at the Armstrong Cross.

Located on the site of the original market cross, erected in 1722 and demolished in 1827, the replacement Grade II-listed memorial Armstrong Cross was unveiled 2 August 1902 by Sir Lowthian Bell. Designed by the architect Charles Clement Hodges in a Celtic-influenced Art and Craft design it was paid for by the friends of Lord and Lady Armstrong of Cragside. Standing at 6.9 metres (22.6 feet) on the faces of the shaft can be found various sculptured representations of wildlife including stags, rabbit's squirrels and birds. The other sides have fine examples of designs including Celtic knotwork and vine scrolls.

38. Stamfordham

The sleepy village of Stamfordham is located 19 kilometres (12 miles) west of Newcastle upon Tyne and is best reached via the B6318 (Military Road) and turning off onto the B6309.

The name Stamfordham is from the Old English, Stannerton meaning 'homestead at the stoney ford'. The ford was a crossing on the River Pont, which runs to the south of the village. The earliest recorded mention of Stamfordham is in documents dating from the year 1188.

Arranged around a long sloping village green, its mainly eighteenth-century buildings are set in two rows, one on the high side of the incline to the north and the other on the low side to the south. They are aptly named as North Side and South Side.

The Grade I-listed Church of St Mary the Virgin is positioned to the west of the green and contains parts of an archway, which may well date from an earlier Saxon church on the site. The majority of the buildings fabric dates from the thirteenth century with a major restoration in 1848 having been carried out under the direction of architect Benjamin Ferrey (1810–1880). While the church contains many ancient artefacts, one of note is the banner of the Order of Bath, which belonged to Arthur Lord Stamfordham and hung in his stall in the Henry VII Chapel in Westminster Abbey. Lord Stamfordham, Sir Arthur Bigge (1849–1931), was the son of the church vicar Revd John Frederick Bigge and spent his childhood in the village. He went on to serve as a private secretary to the royal family for some fifty years, firstly serving Queen Victoria and then George V.

St Mary the Virgin Church.

Market Cross or
Butter Cross.

Standing on the western side of the village green is the Grade II-listed Market Cross, also known as the Butter Cross. A small square sandstone building with open arches on each of its four sides, it was used by farmers' wives on fair days to sell butter and eggs. It was built by Sir John Swinburne of Capheaton in 1735 in times when the village held a weekly cattle market. The building is also classified as a Scheduled Ancient Monument.

To the eastern end of the village green is the Grade II-listed lock-up, which dates from the early nineteenth-century. A single-storey rectangular sandstone building, it has only one door and no windows. Predating the National Police Force, local law breakers would be temporarily held at the lock up before either serving time for their crime or being moved to gaols such as Hexham or Newcastle upon Tyne for trial.

39. Whitton

The small village of Whitton is located to the immediate south of the town of Rothbury, passing over the River Coquet take the road to the right-hand side, signposted to Great Tosson.

The name Whitton is from the Old English 'Hwita's farm/settlement' or alternatively 'White farm'. The village has two towers, one from the fourteenth century and the other built in the eighteenth century, both are Grade II* listed.

The fourteenth century saw the erection of a Vicar's Pele Tower, built to offer protection to both the vicar and local residents from attacks which often occurred throughout Northumberland in those days. In the nineteenth century a Gothic Revival-style rectory was attached to the tower and the building is now a private residence.

Above: Vicar's Pele Tower.

Left: Sharp's Folly.

The second tower in the village is Sharp's Folly (Sharpe's Folly), built in the 1720s by Thomas Sharp, Rector of Rothbury and Archdeacon of Northumberland. Standing at 9 metres (30 feet) the tower was built as an astronomical observatory for Sharp and also to alleviate local unemployment. There must have been something in the Sharp family blood as Thomas's son William built a folly and rock grotto at Hartburn, Northumberland while he was the vicar of the village church.

South

40. Aydon

Aydon Castle is a Scheduled Ancient Monument and Grade I-listed building located 1 mile north of the town of Corbridge, signposted from the B6321 road. There is a car park close to the site entrance and the parking charge is refundable against the entrance fee. The site is managed by English Heritage.

The name Aydon is from the Old English 'heg-denu' meaning 'hay pasture'.

While known as Aydon Castle, technically it is a fortified manor house, the original site having been developed by Robert de Reymes in 1296. He was a wealthy Suffolk merchant who had obtained the Barony of Bolam, which included lands at Aydon. He initially built a manor house but due to the Scottish conflicts and Border Wars decided it prudent to add fortifications. In 1305 he obtained permission from Edward I to crenellate the property, adding battlements and a curtain wall. Despite the fortifications it wasn't sufficient to prevent the Scots from attacking and looting the building in 1315. During 1317 it was the turn of English rebel forces to raid and occupy Aydon and again the Scots in 1346.

Moving forward to more peaceful times on the English-Scottish borders the castle slowly turned into a ruin, but thankfully was restored in the nineteenth century by the then owner Sir Edward Blackett. At that time it was leased to a tenant farmer and was used as a farm up until 1966 when Sir Charles Blackett passed the castle into the guardianship of the Ministry of Works who commenced further restorations.

Now under the management of English Heritage the renovated buildings around the three courtyards are a delight to explore. The site is well signposted with information as to the purpose of the many rooms, but as ever it is advisable to buy a guidebook from the site shop. Many of the original thirteenth-century features such as fireplaces can be seen in a number of rooms, perhaps the grandest being in the first-floor private apartments. Ancillary rooms at ground

Above: Aydon Castle internal view.

Left: Aydon Castle courtyard.

level include kitchens, store rooms and stables, which in later years were used as a cow byer when the site was turned into a farm. The orchard, which overlooks the Cor Burn (stream), was originally the kitchen garden and was planted with fruit trees in 1941. Provided with tables, benches and seats it is an ideal place for a picnic on a sunny afternoon.

41. Blanchland

Located on the border of Northumberland and County Durham, the rural village of Blanchland rests in the Derwent Valley and is part of the North Pennines Area of Outstanding Natural Beauty.

One of the best views of Blanchland can be obtained when entering the village on the B6306 road, which passes over the mid-seventeenth-century stone bridge. The panorama of the quant old grey stone built village can be appreciated from this elevated view point.

Most visitors to the village arrive by car and a car park is provided to the north of the immediate village and is well signposted. The car park is free but donations are welcomed.

In 1165 the Barony of Bolbec granted an area known as Wulwardshope to a religious colony of Norbertian Canons for the founding of a Premonstratensian community. Blanchland Abbey continued until the Dissolution of the Monasteries, when in 1536 it was dissolved on the orders of Henry VIII. Following the dissolution, much of the fabric of the abbey was recycled to build homes within the village and that is one of the reasons for their uniformed grey stone appearance. Parts of the original abbey were incorporated within the Church of St Mary, which became the parish church in 1752. The church is open to public access throughout the year and any visit to Blanchland should include a tour of the building. The abbey gatehouse, built in the fifteenth century, was part of the abbey complex

Blanchland Abbey Gatehouse.

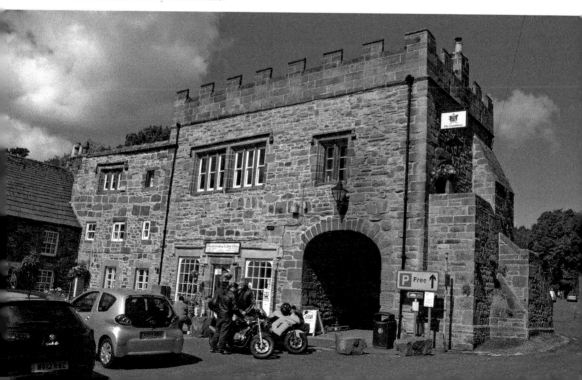

Shildon Engine House.

and is now used as a restaurant in the upper level and Blanchland Shop and post office at ground level. The Lord Crewe Arms is the village's only hotel and pub, but was once part of the abbot's lodge, abbey guesthouse and kitchen. The former quadrangle of the abbey can be seen to the immediate south of the Crewe Arms, with three sides now being occupied by eighteenth-century cottages.

A short walk to the hamlet of Shildon to see the restored engine house is recommended. It is a distance of half a mile: turn left from the car park and follow the lane in a northerly direction. The engine house was built in 1806 to a Cornish style, the only example of its kind in the North East of England and pumped water from Shildon Lead Mine. In the nineteenth century the pump was decommissioned and the building was converted into flats for miners and consequently known locally as 'Shildon Castle'.

42. Chesters Roman Fort

The Grade I-listed Chesters Roman Fort can be reached on the B6318 road; the entrance to the site is on the left if travelling west from the hamlet of Chollerford. Under the guardianship of English Heritage there is a charge for access to the fort and museum.

Claimed to be the most complete Roman cavalry fort in Great Britain, it is well set out on fairly flat ground, falling slowly downhill towards the River North

Tyne. The various buildings such as the headquarters, commanding officer's house, barracks and baths are identified with information boards; however, the purchase of a guide book at the entrance shop is well recommended.

Close by the entrance is the Grade II-listed Clayton Museum, which houses a multitude of Roman artefacts discovered during excavations at Chesters and beyond.

The Roman name for the fort was Cilurnum, which has two meanings: 'cauldron pool' and is also thought to relate to the Cilurnigi people of northern Spain who formed a 500-strong Asturian cavalry unit that was based at Chesters for 200 years. Both suggestions are plausible, given the closeness to the river it could well be that there was an area of disturbance that appeared as a cauldron. It could of course be a mixture of both.

The route of Hadrian's Wall runs from Segedunum Fort in Wallsend in the east to Bowness on Solway to the west, a distance of 117.5 kilometres (73 miles). The wall passed through Chollerford and it was necessary to cross the North Tyne entailing the erection of a bridge, evidence of which can still be seen. Having built a bridge there was a need for a defensive fort to be built to offer protection; however, this is not thought to have been erected until two years after the completion of the bridge and the section of wall. The fort was actively garrisoned with 500 cavalry for at least 200 years before the Roman withdrawal from Britain.

Following the abandonment of Hadrian's Wall, much of the visible stone courses were robbed and used in construction of other buildings. It is often said that most of the present farmhouses on the course of the wall are constructed from such recycled materials. The site returned to agricultural use and lay

Chesters Roman Fort.

Clayton Museum.

untouched and undiscovered for a thousand years, until the investigations of the lawyer and Newcastle town clerk John Clayton (1792–1890). Clayton's father, Nathaniel, had purchased the Chesters estate in 1796. John Clayton had an avid fascination in Roman antiquity and as a result carried out extensive archaeological investigations over more than fifty years at Chesters to once again bring the fort to light. He was also instrumental in the preservation of many other sites along the course of Hadrian's Wall.

43. Corbridge

The market town of Corbridge is located just off the A69 road, 26 kilometres (16 miles) to the west of Newcastle upon Tyne. Popular with tourists, the town caters for the visitor with a number of retail shops, cafés, hotels and public houses. Free car parking is available on the south side of the bridge and it is well signposted – look for 'Corbridge Village Car Park'. The town's railway station is a short distance from the centre.

The town takes its name from its Roman links; the Roman town of Corstopitum lies to the west of Corbridge. Evidence has been translated from Roman writing tablets found at Vindolanda, indicating the town was originally named Coria.

The Grade I-listed bridge at Corbridge has stood since 1674 and was the only bridge to survive on the Tyne during the great flood of 1771, when all others were swept away or damaged. It was not a case of the bridge being so strong that it was able to withstand the force of the flood waters, it was more the fact that to the south of Corbridge is a large flood plain that enabled the river to break its banks and divert around the bridge. The bridge is stone built with seven unequal segmental spans, 147 metres (482 feet) in length; the southern arch was rebuilt in 1829. Widened in 1881, nowadays the bridge carries single-lane traffic.

The oldest building in the town is the Grade I-listed Church of St Andrew's, consecrated in AD 676. It has been suggested that Bishop, and later Saint, Wilfrid may have built the church at the same time as Hexham Abbey. The church is one of the many buildings in Corbridge made of stone recycled from Corstopitum. Pevsner makes the observation that the church is 'the most important surviving Saxon monument in Northumberland, except for Hexham crypt'. The church has been much changed since its origins, as late as 1919 when the south porch was added. Rowan Atkinson, the comedian and actor, donated a decorative glass door for the south porch in 2008 as a memorial to his late mother Ella May.

Standing to the east of the church is the Grade I-listed Vicar's Pele, a thirteenth-century defensive tower that provided housing for the priest at St Andrew's. Being close to the Anglo-Scottish border, the town of Corbridge was often the target of attacks and that is why the vicar required a place of safety. Another building that uses the stones from Corstopitum, it was used as a vicarage until the seventeenth century. In recent years the building has been converted into a micro-pub and brewery.

A popular meeting place, especially for cyclist groups is the Market Cross. The original cross is on display outside of the Pele Tower and carries its own Grade II listing. The base of the cross is claimed to have been taken from a Roman column – the shaft dates from the thirteenth century and the head eighteenth century. Hugh Percy, the Duke of Northumberland, commissioned

Corbridge Bridge.

Vicar's Pele Tower.

a new cross in 1814 that was constructed from cast iron. The quatrefoil shaft supports the cross and is on a stone base with a four-stepped plinth. It is Grade II listed.

44. Featherstone Castle

Located on a plateau at the base of the South Tyne Valley, a public right of way starts at the modern road bridge crossing the River South Tyne on the Coanwood to Lambley road. That path follows the eastern side of the river, passing the former Second World War prisoner of war camp and ending opposite the castle. My interest in this site had been raised when I observed interesting shapes on the ground when using Google Earth to examine the area, the satellite view showing outlines of the former camp buildings and emphasises the extent of its footprint.

The castle stands near to the confluence of the Hartley Burn and the River South Tyne and is Grade I listed. Built in 1212 as a defensive manor house and pele tower for Helias de Featherstonehaugh, the earliest part of that building to survive is a thirteenth-century hall, now incorporated in west range and the south-west tower dating from the fourteenth century. Much of the castellated style was, however, added in the nineteenth century.

The castle became Hillbrow School (boys' preparatory school) in 1950. The school remained there until 1961 when it was converted into a conference and activity centre for students. The castle is not open to the public but good views can be achieved from the pathway at the riverside.

In the Second World War an area to the south of Featherstone Castle was used to construct a training camp, named Camp 18, to house troops from the United

States of America training prior to their deployment in the Normandy Invasions. Despite it lying in the beautiful South Tyne Valley, the soldiers considered the camp to be too isolated and gave it the unfortunate nickname of 'Death Valley'. In 1945 the camp was converted to hold captured German officers, categorised as 'Black Nazis' – they were fervent followers of Hitler's doctrines. It was considered that such prisoners could only safely be repatriated after the end of hostilities after extensive physiological rehabilitation and this they received at Camp 18. Originally the camp had 200 huts, based in four sections and housing 4,000 officers together with 600 orderlies from the lower ranks. The camp also had a chapel, bakery, library, theatre and hospital. In the period 1945 to 1948 there were 25,000 German prisoners of war passing through the camp. The camp closed in 1948.

Featherstone Castle from the south.

Former Second World War camp.

45. Haltwhistle

The town of Haltwhistle lies in the Tyne Valley on the road and rail route between Newcastle upon Tyne and Carlisle.

The name Haltwhistle is often confused as having a direct connection with a railway crossing or stop and, while the town has a long association with rail transport, it is derived from the Old English 'Hautwysel', meaning 'fork of a river by a hill'. Historically, a settlement may have been here since the time of the Roman occupation, a small fort having been discovered at Haltwhistle Burn, a stream that runs through the town.

The town brands itself as being the geographical centre of Britain – based on it lying in the centre of the longest line of latitude running through the country. It is often said that a pin placed under Haltwhistle would enable Britain to be finely balanced. This adds to the tourist appeal of the town, which is on the on the Pennine Way walking route, together with the fact that Hadrian's Wall is within 5 kilometres (3 miles).

The population of Haltwhistle grew with the coming of the railway, when in 1838 the station on the Newcastle to Carlisle line was opened, and again in 1852 when the Alston to Haltwhistle line came into operation. The railway stimulated industrial activity, allowing goods to be transported quicker and further afield. By this time several industries had opened on the banks of the Haltwhistle Burn and surrounding coal mines and quarries were able to increase production. The railway station continues to serve passenger traffic and is much the same as when it was built in 1838. The station house, ticket office and waiting room are designed in a Tudor style by Newcastle Architect Benjamin Green. As a testimony to the days of steam-driven trains, a water tank dating from 1863 remains, designed by

Haltwhistle station view from the west.

Haltwhistle station water tank.

the Newcastle and Carlisle Railway's engineer Peter Tate, and built by R. Wylie & Company. The building is Grade II listed and was restored in 1999. The cast-iron footbridge linking the north and south platforms is also of historical interest. Grade II listed, it was erected in the nineteenth century for the North Eastern Railway. Erected at the same time was the signal box, which is located on the south platform. Another building in the station carrying a Grade II listing, it was given a National Railway Heritage Award in 2003.

46. Haydon Bridge

Lying on both the north and south sides of the River South Tyne is the village of Haydon Bridge. Haydon in Old English means 'hay valley'. It was first recorded in 1309 when there was an inquest into the death of Thomas, Baron of Langley, who was described as living 'apud Pontem de Haydon', loosely translated as next to Haydon Bridge.

A popular place for the passing tourist, the village has a number of hotels and guesthouse accommodation. It is well served to quench the thirst with three pubs – The Anchor, The Railway Hotel and The General Havelock Inn. There is also a working men's club.

Two bridges cross the river in the village centre: the now 'old' Haydon Bridge, dating from 1776, these days used for pedestrians and its replacement; and the modern-day road bridge, which was commenced in 1967 and completed in

1970. The A69 trunk road between Newcastle upon Tyne and Carlisle used to be routed through the village, but a new bypass was opened to the south in 2009, which included a new bridge taking traffic over the river South Tyne. The village now has three bridges.

The 1776 six-arch bridge replaced an earlier one that was severely damaged by the great flood of 1771. The earliest reference to a bridge is in the inquest report mentioned above and it was probable that it was wooden in construction with gates and guards to control passage.

John Sykes, writing in his local records, reported this incident of 21 December 1806:

> About ten o'clock on the morning, one of the arches of Haydon Bridge, about 95 feet in span, which had long shewn evident signs of weakness and decay, fell with a tremendous crash, just at the time a number of people were passing to church. One unfortunate man sunk with the ruins to the depth of forty feet, but was taken out alive, with a broken thigh bone and otherwise much bruised.

During 1967 the old bridge was closed to traffic as it could no longer cope with the weight and size of modern-day vehicles. A temporary bridge was installed while the new road bridge was built, and the new crossing point opened in 1970. The old bridge is Grade II listed and now only carries pedestrian traffic, offering a pleasant walk from one side of the river to the other.

Eighteenth-century bridge.

Pedestrian
walkway.

47. Hexham

Lying to the immediate south of the A69 Newcastle to Carlisle road is the medieval market town of Hexham. Crossing the River Tyne via the Hexham Bridge, there is a large car park accessed on the left-hand side – signposted as 'Wentworth Car Park'. This is an ideal starting point for a wander around the streets of the town. The town is served by a railway station on the Newcastle to Carlisle line.

Historically the first recorded mention of what is now Hexham is in AD 674 when Wilfrid, a former monk of Lindisfarne, later appointed Bishop of York, was awarded land by Queen Etheldreda of Northumberland to build a church and Benedictine monastery. Wilfrid was later canonised as Saint Wilfrid. In AS 681 the settlement is recorded as Hagustaldes ea, meaning 'stream of Hagustad'. In Old English, 'Hagustaldes' ('Hagustad') means 'a young man who has built an enclosure outside of the settlement in which he was born'. At a later date the 'ea' part of the name was changed to 'ham'; translated in Old English as 'homestead'.

The original church was built by Wilfrid between AD 675 and 680. The present rebuilt and extended church is Hexham's most prominent building, dedicated to St Andrew and these days is more usually known as Hexham Abbey. Situated in the centre of the town, it is open to the public and well worth a visit to appreciate the fine Grade I-listed building and its numerous artefacts. The original church was built mainly by overseas craftsmen and from stones recycled from the abandoned Roman fort at nearby Corbridge. Examples of the Saxon church can still be seen within the fabric of the current building including the original crypt.

Close to the east end of the abbey can be found the Saxon Market Place, the medieval Moot Hall and Town Gaol. The Grade I-listed Moot Hall, dating from the fourteenth century, was the seat of the town's courts. It also acted as a gateway and a defensive tower during Hexham's troubled times when the

Hexham Abbey viewed from the Market Place.

Hexham Moot Hall.

town was the subject to Scottish attacks and raids from the North. In 1297 for instance the town was sacked by William Wallace's Scottish army. During the War of the Roses the Battle of Hexham was fought in 1464 to the south of the town. The Lancastrian commander, Henry Beaufort Duke of Somerset, was subsequently beheaded in the marketplace and buried in the abbey.

Markets are still held at the Grade II*-listed Shambles, an open building with Tuscan columns on three sides and wooden posts on the other side, erected by Sir Walter Blackett in 1766.

The Grade I-listed Old Gaol is open as a museum and art gallery. Built in 1330 on the orders of Archbishop Melton of York as a prison, it remained as such into the nineteenth century. It also acted as a defensive tower and is another Hexham building that contains stones from the Roman fort at Corbridge.

48. Lambley

Lambley Viaduct is part of the South Tyne Trail, which is open to the public and a pleasant walk of 3 kilometres (2 miles) from the dedicated car park at Coanwood. Adjacent to the viaduct is a wooden footbridge linking Lambley with Coanwood; it is a good vantage point for viewing the structure from river level. As part of the walk from Coanwood you use the footbridge to cross the river and climb a set of stairs up to the viaduct deck. Unfortunately this is due to the former Lambley railway station being closed off to the public. Originally a footbridge was attached to the piers of the viaduct, but this fell into disrepair in the 1950s and was removed, being replaced with the present bridge.

Lambley Viaduct viewed from the south.

Church of St Mary and St Patrick.

Grade II* listed and built in 1852 to carry the Alston to Haltwhistle railway across the River South Tyne, the design being attributable to the Newcastle upon Tyne-born civil engineer Sir George Barclay Bruce (1821–1908). The span crossing the river is composed of nine arches, measuring 17 metres (56 feet), the total length of the viaduct being some 260 metres (853 feet), and the height of the railway bed is 33 metres (108 feet) above the river. The viaduct fell into disuse in 1976 when the railway line was closed and unfortunately it was allowed to fall into a state of disrepair. Between 1995 and 1996 the viaduct was renovated. Part of the restoration involved the entire viaduct being repointed with lime, which entailed over 3,000 square metres (32,291 square feet) of lime being used that was imported from France.

The village is served by the Grade II-listed Church of St Mary and St Patrick, named after a former twelfth-century Benedictine nunnery at the confluence of the Black Burn and River South Tyne at Lambley, which was destroyed by a flood of the River South Tyne in 1769. The present church replaced an earlier building and was designed by Scottish architect William Searle Hicks (1849–1902); it opened in 1885. The chancel has fine stone vaulting and it is claimed that the church bell originated at the nunnery of St Mary and St Patrick. The Lambley and Hartleyburn war memorial, in the form of a cross of St Cuthbert and made from Aberdeen granite, is located in the churchyard. It is dedicated to the four local men who lost their lives in the First World War (1914–18).

49. Prudhoe Castle

The town of Prudhoe is 18 kilometres (11 miles) west of Newcastle upon Tyne. The castle is located off the A695 road and is well signposted. A free car park is available close to the entrance. The remains of the castle are under the custodianship of English Heritage and open to the public.

The name Prudhoe is from the Old English 'Pruda's hill spur' – Pruda is thought to have been a person's name and the town is set on a spur of land.

From a steep ridge the castle commands a defensive position overlooking the Tyne Valley and is a Scheduled Ancient Monument and Grade I-listed building. The first castle on the site, probably motte and bailey, was constructed in the eleventh century for the D'Umfraville family, Sir Robert de Umfraville having been granted the land by William the Conqueror. Historically the castle is unique in Northumberland as it was the only one never to be captured and occupied by the Scots. It was, however, besieged on two occasions during 1173 and 1174 by King William of Scotland (William the Lion). Perhaps the position of the castle on its high ridge, the north and east sides protected by a steep fall away to the valley floor and the moat to the south and west sides, afforded the castle

Prudhoe Castle external view.

Prudhoe Castle internal view, Manor House and Gateway.

protection against the Scots. However, during the English Civil War it was occupied without any notable resistance by both sides – the Parliamentarians and Roundheads.

Prudhoe Castle appears to have been used as a pawn between the king and its owners, with its ownership changing on several occasions. As was common in medieval times, any failure to align with the English throne resulted in forfeiture of lands or, even worse, execution. Ultimately the castle became the property of the Earls of Northumberland – the Percy family – and it remained so until 1966 when it came under the guardianship of the Crown, although it was still owned by the Percys.

A tour of the castle shows that the curtain wall remains more or less intact, as does the barbican gate and towers to the north-west and south-west. The gatehouse is well preserved and contains a chapel at its upper level. The original keep was demolished in the nineteenth century and only part of one of its walls can still be seen. The keep was replaced with a Georgian manor house between 1808 and 1817, which was designed by Newcastle architect David Stephenson (1757–1819) for Hugh Percy, 2nd Duke of Northumberland. The manor house now holds a visitor centre and exhibition gallery.

50. Shotley

The now redundant Grade II-listed Church of St Andrew's is located just off the A68 Corbridge to Darlington road, taking a left hand turn if travelling from the north onto a minor road signposted for Wittonststall. The church can be seen on the right-hand side of the road in its isolated position on Grey Mare Hill.

The church is under the guardianship of the Church Conservation Trust and is open to the public; access is via a permitted unpaved track running along the side of a field.

The present building erected in 1769 replaced an earlier medieval church, with later restoration and alterations having been carried out in 1892. It closed for religious services on 29 October 1971 and was taken over by the Trust in 1973. The church is built to a crucifix plan and internally the church is quite plain with white painted plastered walls. Retained are some of its nineteenth-century fittings such as window altar, wooden pews and lectern. The segmented rib-arched vault is inscribed with the year '1769'. An interesting piece of history can be seen in the vestry at the north end of the church. A plaque is affixed to the wall that holds a certificate from the Incorporated Church Building Society granting £20 in 1889 towards the rebuilding of the church.

St Andrew's Church.

Hopper Mausoleum.

Dominating the churchyard is the Grade I-listed Hopper Mausoleum, which was erected in 1752 by Humphrey Hopper of Black Hedley in memory of his wife Jane, who died on 29 February 1752 aged seventy-seven. Built from sandstone, the memorial follows a baroque style with its shell-headed niches containing several carved figures, some of which are damaged and others missing. At the front of the tomb is an enclosed forecourt in which two recumbent figures lie next to each other in an arched recess, perhaps meant to represent John and Jane Hopper.

The churchyard also contains several Grade II-listed headstones, one of which is in memory of John Hunter, a blacksmith who died in 1799. The rear face of his headstone has this verse:

> My Anvil and Hammer lies declind
> My Bellows have quite lost their wind
> My Fires extinct my Forge decayd
> My Vice is in the dust all laid
> My Coals is spent my Iron gone
> My Nails are drove my Work is done
> My Mortal part lies nigh this stone
> My Soul to Heaven I hope is gone.